LONDON BUS LIVERIES
A MISCELLANY

MALCOLM BATTEN

AMBERLEY

First published 2019

Amberley Publishing
The Hill, Stroud
Gloucestershire, GL5 4EP

www.amberley-books.com

Copyright © Malcolm Batten, 2019

The right of Malcolm Batten to be identified
as the Author of this work has been asserted
in accordance with the Copyright, Designs and
Patents Act 1988.

ISBN 978 1 4456 9065 0 (print)
ISBN 978 1 4456 9066 7 (ebook)

British Library Cataloguing in Publication Data.
A catalogue record for this book is available from
the British Library.

Origination by Amberley Publishing.
Printed in the UK.

Introduction

London buses are red and have been for over a hundred years. The livery was introduced by the London General Omnibus Company in 1907 and was continued by London Transport on its formation in 1933. It was then perpetuated in principal by its successors after 1985, including after privatisation. Until 1969, there were also green buses operating in the surrounding country areas, and on the cross-London Green Line express routes. However from January 1970 the country area buses and Green Line vehicles were transferred to the National Bus Company as a new company named London Country Bus Services. Therefore they are considered as outside the scope of this book.

While red has been a consistent part of the livery, the application of relief colours and fleetname or symbol design has varied over the years, in line both with fashion and changes of ownership, so this will be examined initially.

From 29 June 1984 London Regional Transport took over control of London Transport from the Greater London Council, which was abolished. Then, from 1 April 1985, a new wholly owned subsidiary, London Buses Ltd, took on the operation of buses.

When route tendering was introduced in 1985, vehicles working on LRT tenders were required to carry the LRT logo, but companies could choose their own colour scheme and fleetname. This brought a wide variety of colours and names to Greater London, even on the streets through the heart of the West End when companies like Grey-Green and Kentish Bus won tenders for some of the trunk routes. In later years new or recent vehicles would usually be specified in these contracts, but initially many of these companies bought former London Transport Daimler Fleetlines, which were being sold off prematurely. However, routes 13 and 19 were worked by London Buses companies with Routemasters and when these routes were won by other operators they took over the existing buses, painting them in their own colours. For space reasons it is not intended to include more than a sample of these tendered operations here. Readers interested in this era are recommended to the author's companion book *London Buses: The Colourful Era 1985–2005* (see bibliography).

London Buses set up some low-cost units to compete for tenders, and some of these units adopted differing liveries, such as Bexleybus who used a blue and cream scheme similar to that of Eastbourne Corporation with whom they had links.

In April 1989 London Buses was split into ten regional operating units, plus the pre-existing London Coaches who ran the sightseeing operation and Stanwell Buses (Westlink). This was in preparation for eventual privatisation in the 1990s. Buses carried the name of the local unit, e.g. East London or London Central, and a local emblem. The companies adopted a standard livery style that had been agreed in 1988 with a grey skirt and thin white band, although some diversion from this standard livery was allowed.

In 1990 there began to be a disagreement between the thinking of LRT and London Buses. LRT wanted all buses running tendered services under its authority to be in a common livery, i.e. red. London Buses did not want this as they felt that if people were to complain about a bus service, they would be blamed, even if it was another company that was running the offending service. In the event other operators were allowed to keep their own liveries (for now at least), but London Buses vehicles had to be red. This meant the end for the Bexleybus blue and cream.

In 1994 it was announced that purchasers of the London Buses companies on privatisation would have to maintain an 80 per cent LT red livery for vehicles working in central London (Zone 1), including the front of the bus. Existing companies with tendered routes in central London, such as Grey-Green and London & Country were permitted to keep their liveries on current contracts, but would have to adopt red on any new contracts won. Any new companies winning contracts into Zone 1 would also need to adopt the red policy.

The London bus companies were sold off for privatisation in 1994–95. It was the original intention that no one purchaser should be able to buy adjacent operating districts, but there was no restriction regarding selling on by the original purchasers. Major national bus-owning groups were emerging by the end of the decade, as a result of takeovers and the selling on of former National Bus Company fleets, some of which had initially gone to management buyouts. Stagecoach was one, Arriva (a re-naming of the Cowie group of companies who owned Grey-Green) was another. First Group and the Go-Ahead Group made up the remainder of the 'Big Four'. All of these groups would eventually acquire one or more of the former London Buses districts, as well as buying up other companies that had won London tendered routes including the successors to London Country Bus Services. Stagecoach, Arriva and First Group all adopted a national livery scheme for their companies outside of London, but because of the LRT 80 per cent rule they could not use these on central London routes. So they adopted versions of a red livery incorporating some of their identifying features. Arriva adopted a red and stone variant of their national turquoise blue and stone livery, although some buses working wholly in the outer suburbs did receive the national scheme.

The new millennium coincided with a change in ownership for London's bus services. From 3 July 2000 a new Mayor of London was appointed, who took over responsibility for London Bus Services Ltd and a new regulatory authority called Transport for London (TfL).

In 2002 it was decreed that all London Bus routes should be worked by 80 per cent red buses, not just those in central London. Then for contracts signed from 1 July 2004 TfL's livery policy was effectively tightened to overall red, with only the fleetname to differentiate the separate companies. Each of the companies gradually dropped their embellishments, with the Go-Ahead Group the last to drop their grey skirt in favour of plain red in 2011.

However despite the degree of control over liveries exercised by London Transport and its successors, over the years there have been several exceptions and variations to the rule. Some routes have featured vehicles with special promotional lettering or liveries. Sometimes this has been to promote routes through central London that were seen as having tourist appeal. In outer London it might be to encourage bus usage in a particular area. Certain routes have been introduced in co-operation with local councils or organisations who have part-funded them, and a livery reflecting this involvement has been applied to the vehicles used on the route. There were also commercial routes outside the main bus network such as the Airbus services linking London and Heathrow Airport.

The Round London Sightseeing Tour was developed from the 1970s with open-top buses as well as a mix of recent vehicles and hired coaches. From 1986 until privatisation Routemasters were deployed on the service – some converted to open-top and all carrying a special promotional livery.

Vehicles have appeared in commemorative liveries for royal and anniversary occasions, including significant anniversaries in the history of transport in London. There have been vehicles painted for special promotions by London Buses or Transport for London such as promoting Oyster cards or the green credentials of hybrid and electric vehicles. Vehicles used on contracts or long-term rail replacement services have also carried special liveries specified by the contractor. Also vehicles used for private hire and tours or for driver training rather than bus routes are not subject to the livery restrictions and have been given separate liveries. Finally, many vehicles have carried commercial advertising liveries on occasion since 1969. However, as these advertising liveries are often short-term and have been comprehensively covered in other books, only a brief coverage of this will be included here.

In a book of this size it is not possible to cover every variant livery style used by London Transport and its successors since 1970 (even if I had photographed them all!) but hopefully a representative selection has been assembled.

All photographs are by the author.

Development of a Standard Livery

London Transport 1970–85

In 1907 the LGOC introduced the 'GENERAL' name on its vehicles, and the following year the familiar red livery was inaugurated. Prior to this, vehicles had been liveried and lettered according to the routes they ran on. When London Transport was formed they kept the red livery. This was later simplified, partially to save money and also because of the introduction of spray painting.

What is perhaps best regarded by enthusiasts and the public alike as a 'standard' livery is that applied to the RT family and the Routemaster family in the 1960s. This livery of red with a cream band and gold underlined fleetname can still be seen in London on some of the Routemasters working heritage route 15. But in 1965 this was supplanted by the adoption of a so-called 'flake grey' band and equal height gold lettering, first applied to RM2128 and then applied to new Central Area red buses and repaints. The grey band was also applied to the new single-deck AEC Merlins and Swifts introduced with the reshaping plan. This shade was in fashion at the time – British Railways had adopted a blue and grey livery for their main line carriages from 1964 onwards. However, from 1972 white would replace grey as the relief colour. The London Transport fleetname was replaced by a solid white roundel symbol from 1974 and white fleet numbers were adopted. The white roundel and fleet numbers were not applied to any of the remaining RT buses, which were finally withdrawn from service in 1979. The only exception was RT2958, retained as a radio trainer and repainted in 1981.

In 1961 new RM664 was delivered in unpainted condition to test how this would wear in service. The silver appearance soon turned shabby and the vehicle gained standard red paint when it went in for overhaul in 1965. Six RMs at Highgate were painted all-red in 1968. In 1981 as part of a cost-saving experiment RM376 was turned out with no white band. In addition, several inside areas were painted rather than covered in rexine, some seat squabs had the leather ends omitted and metal plates were fitted to the floor rather than cork tiles. Thankfully these economies were not perpetuated and RM376 soon gained its white band!

Between the late 1970s and early 1980s some garages unofficially turned out buses with modified liveries as rally show-buses. Most of these were Routemasters given cream bands, gold underlined fleetname and offside route number display – Croydon garage with RM1000, Harrow Weald with RM737. There was quite a rivalry to see who could come up with the best presented bus. However, London Buses Ltd banned this practice in 1985.

The classic London Transport livery as many people will think of it – cream band and gold underlined fleetname. RM5 has been restored to this form as part of the Arriva heritage fleet. Here it is seen on a running day to commemorate 100 years of route 76 on 20 July 2013. Many of the Routemasters on heritage route 15 also carry this livery style as can be seen on the vehicle travelling the opposite way at St Paul's Cathedral.

From 1965 'flake grey' replaced cream as the relief colour. Preserved AEC Merlin MBA539 displays the livery style in which these vehicles were delivered. It was displayed at North Weald Station as part of the Epping Ongar Railway bus rally on 9 September 2018. Note the tiny white fleet number, 'Red Arrow' branding and the coin-box symbols for the flat-fare Red Arrow service. White on blue blinds were used by London Transport for Red Arrow and other express services.

RML2453 sports the white band introduced in 1972 and solid white roundel and white fleet numbers introduced in April 1974. It was at Vauxhall on route 77A on 23 February 1985. When new, this bus would have carried green livery as a Country Area vehicle. It had passed to London Country Bus Services in 1970 and then been bought back by London Transport in the late 1970s. Note the grille below the blind box has been reduced in size to allow a full-width cantrail band – this was a modification made to Routemasters from the mid-1960s.

When the DM and DMS Daimler Fleetlines were introduced in 1971 they initially carried all-over red livery and an outline roundel with the words London Transport. This was superseded by the solid roundel from 1973. DMS2003 was at Waterloo in August 1983.

DMS118-367 were supplied with a white 'tween-decks band on the sides only, this was discontinued on later deliveries. Fleetlines delivered in 1975–76, from DMS1968 and including all of the quieter B20 type, received white around the upper deck windows, which improved their appearance considerably. This style was first trialled on DMS46 in 1974. D2545 was at the long gone Hammersmith Butterwick bus stands on 10 April 1981. The MD class Scania Metropolitans were also delivered in this style, but became plain red on repaint from 1980, as did the Fleetlines.

The Leyland Titan was designed in conjunction with London Transport and, when delivered, T1 carried promotional lettering between the decks. At the 1983 North Weald Rally T1 was on display with its original special lettering restored by Hornchurch garage. The original batches of Titans T1-6 and Metrobuses M1-5 had white around the upper deck windows, the Metrobuses also having black skirt panels. However, production batches of these classes were plain red, M1-605 were delivered with black grilles, M606+ had red grilles.

When the BL and BS classes of Bristol LH buses were supplied in 1975–76 they initially carried a livery of white around the windows. In later life this would be replaced by plain red or the 1988+ standard style with grey skirt and a thin white line below the windows. BS5 has entered preservation and displays the original style when seen at Brighton on the HCVS London–Brighton run in May 2005.

In the early 1980s several bus garages adopted vehicles with modified liveries as rally entrants until the practice was banned in 1985. While most of these were Routemasters given original-style features, there were some exceptions. One of the most unusual was BL1 of Edgware garage, given a cream band and gold underlined London Transport fleetname – features superseded before these buses were built. It was photographed at the London Bus Rally of 18 July 1982, which was held at the Ensignbus premises at Purfleet.

The L class Leyland Olympians continued the pattern of unrelieved red as on the Metrobuses and Titans. L38 passing through Orpington near the station approach on 2 August 1986 shows a feature applied to buses from Fleetlines onwards – the painting of the entrance door yellow.

London Buses 1986–89

A new batch of Ford Transits for Hampstead Garden Suburb route H2 had a variant application of the white band. The earlier Transits had a straight white band. FS29 was photographed at Golders Green Station on 21 March 1986.

RML2387 displays the new roundel style adopted by London Buses in 1987. It also shows the London General district name and their B-type bus emblem above the front offside window. Taken at Putney Bridge Station on 21 February 1989.

In 1987 Leaside District adopted a livery of a black skirt and white 'tween-decks band. This can be seen to advantage on one of the second-hand Volvo Ailsas bought from West Midlands and allocated to Potters Bar garage. Volvo V65 stands at Archway Station on 9 March 1988.

A new standard livery style was adopted by London Buses in 1988 with a white 'tween-decks band and a grey skirt, inspired by the black skirt adopted by Leaside District in 1987. This standard style was to be applied to all vehicle types except Routemasters, which did not get the grey skirt. The livery is portrayed by Leyland Olympian L33 of South London, at the Oxford Circus terminus of the 137A on 5 April 1992. Note that this has received the registration number formerly carried by RM1330.

London Bus Companies 1989–94

London Buses was split into eleven separate operating companies in 1989, plus London Coaches who ran the sightseeing and tours business. Officially they adopted the standard 1988 style of livery. However the companies were given a degree of autonomy in the type of vehicles that they bought and the livery in which they were painted.

East London T653 carries gold lining and lettering rather than the customary white. This was introduced initially on RMCs for new route X15 (see p. 39) but also applied to some Titans and eighteen Leyland Nationals intended for Docklands services. Some of the new Scania buses introduced in 1991 also carried this livery. T653 was captured on route 69 at North Woolwich on 28 February 1991.

A one-off livery was applied to LS27, one of six which had been converted to single doors and coach seating for the Forester service in 1986. They later passed to London Coaches from 1987–89 before being dispersed. This one had been used as a private hire vehicle with London Northern in 1991. Here it waits at East Ham 'White Horse' on route D3 on 9 March 1992.

East London bought 26 Optare Delta-bodied DAF SB220 buses in 1992, which they painted in this attractive red and silver livery. DA23 was at the Ilford, Hainault Street terminus of route 369 on 20 March 1993. They were mostly used on Ilford and Barking local services. The yellow bus behind is from the fleet of Capital Citybus.

Selkent chose Dennis Lance chassis with both Alexander and Plaxton bodywork, each carrying this style of colour scheme. DA13 is one of the 1992 Alexander-bodied batch, seen at Lewisham on 13 March 1994.

To mark the launch of London General two Routemasters, RM89 and RM1590, were painted in 1989 in a pre-war style similar to that worn by some buses in 1983 to mark fifty years of London Transport (see p. 60), but with General fleetnames. They were usually to be found on route 11 as with RM1590 at Broadgate by Liverpool Street Station on 12 June 1989.

London United also marked their launch by repainting RML880, the prototype RML in this livery and renumbering it as ER880, its original intended number. It is shown here at a rally in 1994.

London United also painted M1069 in this pre-war style livery in 1989. It was working on route 285 at Hatton Cross Station on 28 April 1990.

Low-cost units

The first of London Buses' low-cost units, Stanwell Buses (trading as Westlink) took over routes 116, 117 (merged with 116) and 203 from 9 August 1986 using existing Leyland Nationals. While the basis of the livery was London red, white and blue bands were added. LS206 arriving at Staines on 6 November 1986 shows the original livery design, which was later modified.

The later style of Westlink livery is displayed on Leyland Titan T971 at Kingston Bus Station on 4 April 1992. These were the first double-deckers for Westlink, acquired when route 131 was won on tender in 1990.

Westlink was the second London Buses company to be privatised when it was sold to its management in January 1994. It was then sold on West Midlands Travel twelve weeks later, and sold again to London United in 1995. A revised livery by designer Ray Stenning was applied to some of their Metroriders from 1996, as seen here on MRL193 in Kingston.

A tendering scheme for the Orpington area in 1985 saw new local minibus routes R1–6 introduced from 16 August 1986. They were won by a new London Buses low-cost unit called Orpington Buses, trading as Roundabout, who adopted a maroon and grey livery. All of the Roundabout vehicles were new minibuses, but three different makes were used. Roundabout RH5 Owl was a 1986 Iveco 49.10 with a Robin Hood twenty-one-seat body is seen at Orpington Station on 28 August 1986. When new vehicles replaced these they were in standard red livery.

A tendering scheme for the Harrow area saw another London Buses low-cost unit formed. Harrow Buses started on 14 November 1987 with a mix of new and second-hand vehicles. A red and cream livery was adopted. The new vehicles were leased MCW Metrobus 2s such as M1470 taken in South Harrow on 26 March 1988. The Harrow routes came up for tender again in 1990, and on this occasion only routes 183, H12/4/5 and new route H18 were retained. These routes now came under Metroline using standard red and the Harrow Buses fleetname. The leased MCW Metrobus 2s were returned to their dealer.

When routes in the Woolwich/Bexley area were tendered, the Selkent district general manager negotiated a new low-cost unit working out of a reopened Bexleyheath garage. Eastbourne Corporation had an existing working relationship with Selkent and their blue and cream livery was chosen for the new Bexleybus operation. Bexleybus used a mixture of second-hand and new buses. Thirty-one ex-LT Daimler Fleetlines were sourced, of which fourteen were bought back from Clydeside Scottish. No. 98 (ex-DMS2112) was at Bexleyheath on 15 March 1989. This has the fleetname between decks – the former Clydeside examples had it placed below the lower-deck windows.

The Bexleybus livery fell afoul of new LRT regulations in 1990 that all LRT companies should be red, and as the Fleetlines were replaced by more modern Titans, most of these retained their red livery as seen here at Woolwich. When the routes came up for re-tendering in 1990, virtually everything was lost to other operators. Bexleyheath garage and many of the routes passed to London Central from 24 November 1990. The leased blue and cream Leyland Olympians were returned to their dealer.

Suttonbus was another London Buses low-cost unit, which commenced from 26 November 1988. The livery was basically red, but a mushroom skirt was applied rather than the usual grey. DMS Fleetlines were the main vehicles used except for some Metroriders on new route 352. DMS2293 was loading outside Croydon's Fairfield Halls on 16 August 1989. D2589 also received a yellow 'tween-decks band, although this was not adopted in the final version of the livery.

Post-privatisation, 1994+

The ten main London Buses companies plus Stanwell Buses (Westlink) and London Coaches (already sold) were all privatised in 1994–95. As they all ran into the central London Zone 1, where 80 per cent red was specified, they all retained the red livery but chose to interpret it in differing ways to stress their separate ownerships. The LT roundels were ordered to be removed following privatisation. Subsequently, the main bus-owning companies that had arisen nationally bought into these companies, if they did not already have a presence in London. Because of the red ruling, they could not apply their national liveries but adapted their logos and flashes to fit. Eventually even these would fall foul of the tightened livery code such that now only the fleetnames distinguish different companies.

At first there were a number of experiments with livery styles before the companies settled on a design. One that didn't get adopted was this Metroline version on RML2737 with blue mudguards and wheel hubs. Seen in Oxford Street on 3 August 1995.

Another Metroline experiment was on RML2634 also seen in Oxford Street in 1995.

The final version adopted by Metroline was one of the most attractive seen on a Routemaster. RML2431 rounds Marble Arch on 19 October 1995.

Before adopting blue, Metroline also initially experimented with other skirt colours, as seen here with green on M1035 at the Cobham Gathering rally on 9 April 1995. M326 was given a maroon skirt.

Metroline Dennis Trident/Alexander TA74 shows how on modern buses the blue skirt came about halfway up to the windows but the 'tween-decks band was omitted. This was at Marble Arch on 15 August 1999. The livery was designed by Ray Stenning of 'Best Impressions'. A few vehicles received a pale blue skirt in 2006, but the darker blue shade was then reinstated until dropped altogether after 2009.

MTL London Northern chose plain red, which looked particularly drab on their Routemasters as even the 'tween-decks band was not picked out in another colour. This example has also suffered the indignity of losing the RM prefix to its number and being reregistered, although at least it retains the chromework around the radiator – some had this painted over. RM29 was at Golders Green on 18 March 1996. MTL London sold out to Metroline in 1998.

This experimental livery was applied to London United M1238, as seen at a rally in 1995, but was not adopted.

London United adopted this livery style with white (originally a very pale grey) upper deck and roof and grey skirt, which considerably brightened up their vehicles. Alexander-bodied Volvo Olympian VA7 was at Raynes Park on 6 July 1996. Routemasters, however, were painted in a more traditional style with a 'tween-decks grey band and grey wheel hubs. The fleetname and logo were placed between decks at the front of the advert panels.

Stagecoach chose to paint their Routemasters with a traditional cream band and the fleetname in gold. RML2671 stands at Paddington on 11 April 1995.

When Stagecoach first bought East London and Selkent, buses other than Routemasters (and those in special route branded liveries) were painted plain red with white fleetnames. VN307 (M307 DGP) was a Volvo Olympian with Northern Counties body seen on route P3 in Peckham Rye on 23 September 1997.

From 2001 onwards the national Stagecoach livery was amended to replace the coloured *Starsky & Hutch* stripes with softer curves and a new logo. A London version was devised to meet the 80 per cent red requirement for the central area. Dennis Trident/Alexander TAS455 unloads at Romford market on 10 November 2001.

First Bus bought CentreWest from its management in 1997, which gave them a presence in London. The 'Londonised' version of their later corporate livery is seen on a Dennis Trident at Euston Station on 24 March 2004. The Routemasters retained a more restrained style. First Bus later sold their London bus operations to Tower Transit.

Cowie Leaside experimentally painted M533 with blue diagonal bands towards the rear and a stripe above the radiator grille. However they then adopted a yellow version in 1995, as seen on M765 at Edmonton on 13 April 1996. The Routemasters retained a more restrained style in keeping with their design with a white or yellow 'tween-decks band.

The Cowie Group was renamed Arriva in October 1997. The Leaside, South London and Grey-Green names were dropped in favour of Arriva Serving London. The 'Londonised' version of the Arriva livery was promptly nicknamed 'cowhorns' when it appeared. Alexander-bodied DAF DLA8, seen outside the Prudential building in Holborn on 20 March 1999, was one of the first generation of fully accessible double-deck buses to enter service in London. Routemasters retained a traditional style.

Some vehicles not entering the central area, where the 80 per cent red livery (including the front) applied, received a variant version of the national turquoise and stone livery but with red rather than turquoise. L119 YVK, a Northern Counties-bodied Dennis Dart acquired with the Kentish Bus business, was seen near Enfield Town Station on 17 April 1999.

Some vehicles working on suburban routes that did not enter central London did receive the national-style turquoise and stone livery. London & Country won the contract for route 85 but by the time these new Northern Counties-bodied DAF DB250s arrived in May 1998, the company had become part of Arriva and the new livery introduced. The strapline read 'Arriva serving Surrey & West Sussex'. R204 CKO leaves Putney Bridge Station for Kingston on 30 May 1998. These later passed to London United and received their red and white livery.

The Go-Ahead Group acquired London Central and London General, and subsequently also Docklands Buses, Blue Triangle and Metrobus. They adopted a dark grey skirt and thin yellow band until this was dropped in 2011. They were the last company to go to all-over red. London Central Enviro 400 E51 displays the style when new at North Greenwich Station in March 2007.

The current TfL standard. Stagecoach 12423 an Alexander Dennis E40H with AD Enviro440H (MMC) body at Crossharbour terminus on the Isle of Dogs in February 2019. Alongside can be seen a vehicle from the Tower Transit fleet. Only the fleetname and logo, in approximately the same place, differ in their liveries. TfL have reclaimed the roundel and indeed it is now applied to all forms of transport in which they have an interest, including on taxi stand signs and the Woolwich Ferry.

Ex-London Transport Buses with Other Companies who Won Route Tenders

Several of the companies who won routes in the first rounds of route tendering bought former LT Fleetlines, which were being disposed of at the time via Ensignbus. Ensignbus themselves, Cityrama, London Buslines and Metrobus all ran them. Metrobus OUC 52R was formerly DM2052 and was photographed at Bromley North Station on 28 August 1986. Metrobus would later be acquired by the Go-Ahead Group. Their livery gained increasing amounts of red as the rules tightened and now the name is just retained as a secondary fleetname i.e. Go-Ahead Metrobus.

Two companies won tenders for routes that were operated by Routemasters and took over the existing vehicles to operate them. They were Borehamwood Travel Service (BTS) who took route 13 and Kentish Bus who took route 19 Finsbury Park–Battersea Bridge from 24 April 1993. Their RMLs received the Kentish Bus livery and very smart they looked too, with route details and no advertising. RML2452 is at Hyde Park Corner on 30 April 1993.

Route Promotional Liveries

Central London Tourist Routes

Shop-Linker was introduced on 7 April 1979. It was a circular service from Marble Arch to Oxford Street, Regent Street, Knightsbridge and Kensington. Sixteen Routemasters carried this livery, some with sponsored advertising. Originally the route number box displayed the flat fare of 30p, but this was removed after passengers confused the buses with those on route 30. The route was not successful and was withdrawn after September 28. RM2207 was at Hyde Park Corner on 9 June.

In 1984 some Routemasters on route 23 were given 'tween-decks promotional advertising displaying the tourist locations served by the route, the only one serving Tower Hill. RML 2437 passes this location on 22 September 1984.

From May 1985 route 23 became the 15 and continued to be promoted as a tourist route. Upton Park garage painted six RMLs with yellow roofs as a local initiative. This is seen to advantage on RML2527 as it waits on the stand outside Paddington Station on 17 May 1985.

The all-yellow roofs did not find favour with LT management, but a yellow strip on the roof and route branding was applied to three buses including RML2402. Note the yellow section on the blinds indicating that this is on the route 15A variant routed via The Bank of England rather than Tower Hill. It was seen at Ludgate Hill on 31 May 1985. Yellow cantrail bands and route branding were subsequently applied to Routemasters on other central London routes including the 6, 8, 25 and 53.

A new 'Bus It' campaign to promote tourist routes was introduced in 1988 on several Routemaster routes plus the Titan-operated route 25. South London RML2360 displays promotion for route 137 listing two of the key places served – Oxford Circus and Sloane Square. It was proceeding up Park Lane towards the former on 15 April 1989.

Some London Buses Routemaster operated routes were given route branding, but South London went a stage further by adopting this red and cream livery for their route 159 in 1994. A very early Routemaster, RM6 heads down Whitehall on 12 February 1994. Route 159 would become the last to operate Routemasters, the final day being 9 December 2005. However by then vehicles were in standard red. South London had been sold to the Cowie Group who in turn became Arriva in 1997 and adopted standard red livery, in line with the 80 per cent red diktat by then in force.

London General RML2517 has dedicated promotion for route 11 showing several of the key places served, both on the front panel by the blind box and on the sides above the lower-deck windows. Taken in Whitehall on 29 March 1994.

London Central RM1104 at Paddington with the second of the promotional styles used on route 36, which was also adopted for route 12. 2 May 1995.

From 1997 Routemasters on Arriva route 38 gained route branding with this large 38 on the sides. In 1999 they also gained lettering to promote the fact that they passed Sadler's Wells Theatre, which had recently re-opened. RML884 passes Green Park on 11 May.

Routemaster RML2476 on route 23 passes Trafalgar Square on 27 May 1999. Part of the First Centrewest fleet it carries Gold Arrow branding as well as promotional branding for the route.

London United Routemaster RML2702 rounds Marble Arch with promotional branding for route 94, 14 March 2001.

Local Promotions

From 29 October 1983 route 177 Express started. Running Monday–Friday from Thamesmead to County Hall with an express section from Woolwich to Elephant & Castle, the service carried passengers into town in the morning and back in the evening during rush hour. Two Titans, T112–3, were given a special livery and renumbered TE112–3. They appeared at the Aldenham Works Open Day on 25 September 1983.

London General introduced these small Volkswagen City Pacer buses to the streets of central London on route C2 Waterloo–Kensington in 1987. They were branded as Central Hoppa and carried the names of the key places passed including Victoria and Harrods. D339 JUM was on the stand outside Waterloo on 3 July 1989.

When midibuses (as London Buses called them) were introduced widely in 1980s, the operating companies chose different brand names to promote them including East London Hoppa, Midilink (London Northern) and Streetline (London General). There would also be localised names for individual routes or groups of routes such as E Line in Ealing (later changed to Ealing Buses) or U Line (Uxbridge). Renault/Wright RW50 was in Greenford in September 1990.

First Centrewest replaced Routemasters on routes 28 and 31 initially with Mercedes 811D midibuses in 1989 and then in turn with these Dennis Darts with Wright bodies. Both types carried Gold Arrow branding and a list of the places served that were common to both routes. DW22 passes through Kilburn Park on 25 March 1991.

Route 100 was introduced in 1989 to link the City of London with Wapping, an area once dominated by docks and warehouses but now being gentrified as they were converted to posh apartments. MRL129 carried a modest form of route branding. It is seen outside Broadgate – the development that replaced Broad Street Station on 12 June 1989.

The X15 was introduced in March 1989 as an express peak-hours route linking the new housing developments in Beckton with central London. It was worked by RMCs, the former Green Line Routemaster coaches. They had not seen passenger use with London Transport since being acquired back from London Country, instead being used for training. East London gave them this attractive gold lining and later they received names. RMC1513 arrives at Beckton on the evening of 12 July. They were replaced on the X15 by Titans in November 1991, but then worked alongside RMLs on the 15.

Route 607 was introduced as a limited-stop service along the Uxbridge Road between Shepherds Bush and Uxbridge, paralleling route 207. Originally worked by Metrobuses, in late 1991 these were replaced by former Red Arrow Leyland National 2s (converted to single door and fitted with coach seats) and the Lynxes formerly operating on route 128. National 2 LS495 was seen near Uxbridge 21 February 1994.

Red Express route X43 started on 22 June 1992, taking advantage of the new Red Route restrictions on Archway Road to provide a limited-stop peak-hour service between North Finchley and London Bridge. Scania S15 was photographed near Angel, Islington, on 15 March 1993. The buses were also used on other Potters Bar garage routes, including the 84 and 310 into Hertfordshire. Like many of the route-branded liveries featured here this was designed by Ray Stenning of Best Impressions.

Route 88 gained new Volvo B10B/Northern Counties buses in 1993 with Clapham Omnibus lettering – another Ray Stenning design. VN11 was at Piccadilly Circus 15 May 1993. They were replaced by double-deckers in 1997, but without the route branding.

London Northern bought Dennis Darts with Northern Counties bodywork for route C2 and branded them with C2 Camden Link lettering in 1994. DNL107 was at Parliament Hill Fields on 30 June 1994. This route replaced the northern end of Routemaster-worked route 53.

Route 607 was double-decked in 1996 with these Northern Counties-bodied Volvo Olympians. A revised livery style with white between the decks was applied with route branding thereon. This was later removed in favour of commercial advertising. Note the white on blue blinds – traditionally used by LT and its successors for limited-stop routes. Taken in Hanwell in October 1996.

An unusual situation arose in 1997 when CentreWest received three Plaxton-bodied Dennis Dart SLF buses, L237–9, for route 105. The route had been won from London & Country in 1996 and these were to replace East Lancs-bodied Darts on loan from London & Country. They were delivered in a version of L&C livery but without the red stripe. L238 appeared at the Brooklands Gathering rally before entering service.

Route 371, operated by London United, was treated to route branding in 1997. The buses each carried a different slogan. Optare Excel XL1 loads in Eden Street, Kingston, on 21 July 1997.

Another London United-worked route to get the branding treatment was the 216. This Wright-bodied Dennis Dart was photographed in Richmond on 16 June 1999. Note that on this occasion the bus is actually working route H22 rather than its intended route.

Back north of the Thames, route 83, Golders Green–Ealing Hospital, received local promotion when twenty Northern Counties-bodied Volvo Olympians arrived in 1999 – the last non low-floor double-deckers for London. Challenger was a brand name for First Bus routes from Alperton garage. VN90 waits at Golders Green, 17 September 1999.

New feeder routes for the Croydon Tramlink, introduced in 2000, were worked by First Bus from their Orpington garage. Marshall-bodied Dennis Dart SLFs were used painted in this red and white style to match the livery of the Croydon trams at that time. DML375 was at Addington Village interchange on 18 May 2000.

From May 2017, TfL introduced a six-month trial to see if dedicated route branding would increase ridership. The seven routes that serve Barkingside were selected with about 75 per cent of the buses on each route being branded. The branding was also applied on bus stops and maps, each route having a different colour. The nearsides show route details rather than advertising. Arriva T177 displays the style for route 150 at Barkingside on 1 June.

Hayes area routes were also treated in 2018. Only around one third of the vehicles on each route received the branding, which was a different colour for each route. Abelio AD E20D 8878 carries the green branding for route 195 and was seen in Hayes during April 2018.

Locally funded initiatives

Route 128 was introduced in 1977 with the financial support of Hillingdon Council. At first, Bristol LS buses were used in standard red but with yellow window surrounds rather than white and small lettering below saying 'Hillingdon Local Service'. Later a bolder style was applied as on BL95 seen arriving at Showbus, Woburn, on 4 September 1983.

The Bristols were later replaced by Leyland Nationals in a dedicated red and yellow livery from 13 July 1988. These in turn were replaced by Leyland Lynx buses in the same colours, two of which were bought by Hillingdon Council and operated by London Buses. LX1 emerges from Uxbridge garage on 8 July 1989. Route 128 ended in August 1991, replaced by an extension to route U1.

From 3 January 1983 a new D1 Docklands Clipper route started, linking Mile End Station with the new financial quarter being created on the Isle of Dogs by the London Docklands Development Corporation, who financially supported the route. Running every 15 minutes, six Leyland Nationals with route branding were used. On this occasion one of the Docklands Clipper-liveried buses has strayed onto route 108 and was observed at Lewisham. 2 August 1986.

New route C3 was introduced from 13 April 1987 to link Earls Court Station with the new Chelsea Harbour luxury housing development. It was worked by London Coaches on behalf of LRT. Four minibuses were used: two Ivecos and two Freight Rover Sherpas. All were painted in a blue livery. This was probably chosen as the route ran close to the Chelsea football ground, whose team play in blue. The route was later extended to Clapham Junction and converted to double-deck vehicles in normal red livery. Freight Rover Sherpa D585 OOV was at Earls Court on 11 February 1989.

A rather more modest promotion for routes G1 and G2 was introduced in 1988 and was supported by Wandsworth Health Authority. Not a separate livery, but the WHA branding was applied to the MCW Metroriders that worked the services. Note also the Wandle District waterwheel logo by the entrance door. SG5 was passing through Wandsworth Common on 3 September 1988. SG1–6 were soon after renumbered MR93–8.

Westlink route H20 was a new route developed in partnership with Hounslow Council in 1989. Three wheelchair-accessible CVE Omni buses were employed, one in Westlink colours and two in this white Hounslow livery. This was taken on the route on 10 May 1989.

An initiative funded by Hounslow Council saw routes H24 and H25 worked by wheelchair-lift-equipped Iveco minibuses in this livery and branded as Hounslow Hoppa. London United FR1 was at Feltham on 19 August 1991. These routes had replaced former Fountain Coaches route 600, which had been surrendered in 1990.

The E5 minibus route, which replaced parts of routes 105 and 120 in Southall from 26 November 1988, used Mercedes-Benz vehicles fitted with wheelchair lifts. The route was partly funded by Ealing Council and the buses carried this special livery variant to denote the fact. MA5 was in Greenford on 26 March 1994, MAs having replaced the original shorter MT class.

New Docklands Express route D1 was introduced in September 1990 linking Canary Wharf with London Bridge and Waterloo stations. It was financially supported by the London Docklands Development Corporation as had been the previous route D1 in 1983. London Forest won the contract and used Titans in branded livery. These passed to East London when London Forest was disbanded in November 1991. T840 is seen out of service at Marsh Wall on the Isle of Dogs with the Docklands Light Railway viaduct behind. New Scania buses later took over this route and the new route D11 with similar branding. 21 November 1991.

BAA, owners of Heathrow Airport, were keen to encourage the use of public transport by both the public and staff. Freeflow Heathrow was introduced in April 1995 as a travel awareness campaign, coupled with improvements to local bus services and route branding. Route 285, Kingston–Heathrow via Hatton Cross, was treated to a new Ray Stenning-designed livery from October 1994 and increased in frequency and operating hours, leading to a dramatic increase in passenger usage. This livery style then inspired the London United fleet livery. M813 displayed the new branding at a rally at Syon Park on 11 September 1994. Some Dennis Darts were similarly branded for the route.

Route A10 was introduced in August 1996 between Uxbridge and Heathrow Airport via the new Stockley Park industrial estate. Sponsorship came from BAA, the London Borough of Hilingdon and Stockley Park. It was worked by First Uxbridge Buses with Dart SLFs in a dedicated livery, again designed by Ray Stenning. L4 was at Heathrow on 22 October 1996.

On 20 February 2010 the £25.8 million East London Transit began. This consisted of two routes. One of which was the EL1 Ilford–Barking–Thames View Estate, the other was EL2, which continued to Dagenham Dock – an area being redeveloped at the time. The routes replaced the 369 and part of the 179. Volvo B9TL buses were provided by Go-Ahead Blue Triangle in a special livery. WVL342 was traversing the Thames View Estate when new.

From 18 February 2017 Go-Ahead Blue Triangle started to put LT class new Routemasters onto the East London routes of EL1 and EL2. They also worked on newly gained route EL3 (formerly numbered 387), Little Heath–Barking Riverside. This was the first application of the type to routes not serving central London. From August the LTs started receiving a version of the route branding that had been applied to their predecessors. LT950 displays the new look in Barking town centre on 14 August.

Commercial and Special Routes

On 2 August 1986 London Buses introduced commercial route X99 from Harlow to Basildon marketed as The Forester. Leyland Nationals were used, re-seated with coach seats and painted in this dedicated livery. LS71 was displayed at Showbus, Woburn on 7 September. Operated without subsidy, it competed with Eastern National route 151 for part of the route, although the 151 was withdrawn after 26 October. Route X99 only lasted for six months, being withdrawn from 7 February 1987.

Limited-stop commercial Airbus routes A1 and A2 were first introduced in November 1980. These replaced the British Airways service between Heathrow and Victoria. Initially just the word Airbus and the roundel were displayed. M1006–29 were the second batch of Metrobuses on the route, fitted with coach seats on the upper deck, replacing the original ones in 1984. M1020 was at Heathrow Airport Terminal 4 on 7 February 1988.

In 1992 the Airbus livery was revised. A grey skirt was incorporated and there were two yellow bands as well as yellow lettering. M1006 here does not have a roundel although some other vehicles did include this. The interiors were also refurbished, the work being carried out by Hants & Dorset Trim Ltd. Taken at Heathrow on 21 June 1992.

In 1995 London United bought twelve Alexander Royale-bodied Volvo Olympians with air conditioning to replace the Metrobuses on the Airbus services. Originally in a similar livery style to the previous picture, but now carrying a later style of Toshiba-sponsored lettering, N126 YRW picks up at Hyde Park Corner on 3 July 1998.

Airbus Direct was a commercial service operated by London United from July 1995 from Heathrow to various hotels in central London. Up to thirty-five Dennis Darts were used, such as DT10, seen in Whitehall on 16 July 1995.

First CentreWest began a new Hotel Express service in 1998 connecting Paddington Station (terminus of the new Heathrow Express trains) with major West End hotels. Four of these silver Marshall-bodied Dennis Darts were used. DML250 was at Paddington on 14 August 1998.

London United started limited-stop services T123 and T4 between Heathrow terminals and a rebuilt Feltham Station in 1999 with new Dart SLFs. A T123 leaves Heathrow on 28 March 1999. The routes were withdrawn by December 2001, replaced by a more frequent service on the 285.

London Buses began operating a clockwise hourly inter-station Carelink service from 21 March 1988 using three leased Volkswagen City Pacers fitted with wheelchair lifts. Connections were made with the Airbus services (that could also carry wheelchairs) at Victoria and Euston. Note the bus stop also shows the main stopping points. OV51 was at Liverpool Street Station on 24 March 1992, by which time the vehicles had become operated by London General. From October 1992 the service passed to F. E. Thorpe and was relaunched as Stationlink in January 1993.

Non-TfL Routes

The London Buses companies set up in 1989 and the privatised companies that succeeded them have been free to tender for routes outside the TfL area. Any such routes won are not restricted by TfL's livery specifications.

Heathrow is served by some routes that originate outside the TfL area and so are tendered by the local authorities from those areas. In 1993 London United won routes 555–7 on Surrey tenders. Eleven Dennis Dart SLFs (new in 1999) carried this livery style designed by Ray Stenning. DP31 was at Hatton Cross Station on 24 April 1999 in the company of a Dart from London Buslines.

Metroline's Potters Bar garage is situated outside Greater London in Hertfordshire and works routes 84 East Barnet Station–St Albans and 242 under Hertfordshire contracts. The Alexander Dennis Dart buses used on these carry this red, white and blue livery. Although the 84 reaches New Barnet Station, where DEL854 is seen in 2017, travel restrictions are applied on the use of TfL Oyster cards and passes on this route.

Sightseeing

After trialling open-top buses hired from East Kent in 1972 and then hiring open-top former Midland Red BMMO D9s from Obsolete Fleet, London Transport bought seven convertible Daimler Fleetlines from Bournemouth Corporation in 1977. By 1983 only one of the DMO class remained operational. This was DMO3 Stockwell Princess, which was used to provide open-top rides at various depot open days held as part of the 50th anniversary celebrations. Here it is seen at the Stamford Brook garage open day on 4 June. A Southend Corporation Leyland PD3 shares the duties.

M1046 was one of the then new MCW Metrobuses used on the Round London Sightseeing Tour from 1984. However on 26 April 1985 it had strayed onto bus route 11 when spotted at Hammersmith. With competition from other operators London Transport decided to rebrand the RLST as 'The Official London Transport Sightseeing Tour' in 1984, as seen here. Unfortunately some of the other rival operators simply pasted the word 'Official' on their vehicles too.

The Thames Barrier, designed to prevent London from tidal flooding, opened in 1984. A visitor centre was provided, and London Transport provided a shuttle service from Greenwich. Two Fleetlines, DM948 and DM1102, were used after having been converted to open top and named (in 1985) *Royal Eagle* and *Royal Daffodil* – they were former tourist boats that plied the Thames. DM1102 was seen in a revised version of the livery with a yellow band. It was on private-hire duties at Wembley in March 1987.

Open-top Routemaster RM1864 crosses London Bridge on 18 March 1990 in the first style of livery, applied when these were placed on the tour in 1985.

A revised advertising style, indicating some of the key locations passed was applied to vehicles. It was first applied to the ERMs (extended RM) class of ten open-top buses in 1990. ERM 80 crosses London Bridge on 26 May 1990.

Commemorative Liveries

For HM the Queen's Silver Jubilee in 1977, twenty-five Routemasters were repainted in silver, and renumbered as SRM 1–25. They were individually sponsored and carried exclusive adverts for their sponsor inside and out, as well as wool carpets. They were launched at an event in Hyde Park on 10 April, where SRM 18 (ex-RM1906) is seen with sponsorship by National Westminster Bank. They were all taken off for repainting by the end of November. RM2 was painted silver in advance to promote the scheme to potential sponsors.

First Bus repainted RM1650 as SRM3 in 2004, the identity it carried in 1977 (although with different adverts then). It was seen in Oxford Street on route 7 on 3 June 2004. After the withdrawal of Routemasters from normal service this was retained and used on heritage route 9.

In 1979 London Transport marked 150 years of London Buses with a series of events and special liveries. Twelve Routemasters were painted in the livery of Shillibeer's original horse bus of 1829 and also DMS2646 (the highest numbered example, sponsored by British Leyland). RM2142 and the DMS are seen at a rally held in Battersea Park on 15 April 1979. RCL2221, by now converted into a mobile cinema bus for London Transport, was similarly painted, as was RM2, which was used to promote to potential sponsors.

The royal wedding of Prince Charles and Lady Diana Spencer on 29 July 1981 was marked by eight sponsored Routemasters painted in this 'wedding gift' livery. A ninth, RM490, was painted to promote the livery to sponsors and was displayed at the North Weald Rally on 31 May.

In 1983, fifty years of London Transport were celebrated. Four Routemasters – RM8, 17, 1933 and 2116 – were given pre-war-style liveries in slight variations. RM17, seen here at Victoria Station on 7 July, was the only one with black cab window surrounds. Two months later these had been repainted white like the other examples.

DM1933 of Thornton Heath garage was similarly treated, and how much better it looked than in the plain red colour that most of the class carried! Note also the Wandle District logo below the upper rear window. It was exhibited at the North Weald Rally on 22 May 1983.

Red Arrow Leyland National 2 LS438 received this special livery and the name *City Belle*. Photographed at Waterloo on 17 October 1983.

Appropriately enough RM1983 was selected for commemorative treatment and was given gold livery. It was seen at an open day at Stamford Brook garage on 4 June 1983, one of many special events held during the year. It retained the livery until early 1984.

T747 was also given this gold livery, advertising lettering for Leyland, and was renumbered T1983. It was used on sightseeing tours and was recorded at Victoria on 7 July 1983.

D2629 was given this special Croydon Tramways livery to celebrate the Croydon Charter centenary as well as the fifty years of London Transport. This was photographed at the Showbus Rally of 1983, held at Woburn.

Another vehicle given special treatment in 1983 was M57 in this pre-war 1933 General style. It was displayed at the open day held at Chiswick Works on 2 July. The Croydon Tramways-liveried D2629 is alongside. T66 was painted in a similar style to M57.

In 1986 the centenary of West Ham Corporation (now part of Newham) was celebrated by the painting of T613 in this tram-inspired livery. The lettering on the side read 'This vehicle has been repainted by London Buses Forest District and is sponsored by the London Borough of Newham to celebrate the West Ham Centenary 1886–1986'. It was exhibited at Showbus at Woburn on 7 September 1986.

In 1989 LS431, part of the Westlink fleet, was given this livery to celebrate the centenary of Surrey County Council. It was working on LT route 216 at Staines on 10 October 1992. Westlink also worked some Surrey-tendered routes at the time.

Selkent had Olympian L136 repainted in this period livery in 1990 to mark the centenary of the first tram operation in Lewisham. It was allocated to Plumstead garage and was noted in Whitehall on the No. 53 on 17 May 1993.

RMC1461 was restored to original appearance and Green Line livery in 1994. Although painted primarily for display purposes, it also saw use on route 15, as here at Paddington on 23 August 1995. When the route eventually lost its Routemasters in 2003, RMC1461 was donated to Cobham Bus Museum.

Fifty buses (including fifteen Routemasters) were given gold paint or vinyl livery to mark the Queen's Golden Jubilee in 2002. London United TA224 was one of these and was seen in Kingston. Each carried advertising by a sponsor – this carries (appropriately) adverts for Celebrations chocolates.

Also painted gold was London Transport Museum's RT4712. Along with Arriva RM6, by then part of the heritage fleet, it was on display at the Ash Grove garage open day in April 2017. When first painted in 2002 the RT had a white band and TfL fleetname. The band changed to purple in 2003 to mark the fiftieth anniversary of the coronation.

In August 2003 Stagecoach painted RML 2456 in its original London Transport country green livery for the last day of Routemasters on route 15. It then was put to work on surviving RML route 8 (despite the red edict). On 30/31 May 2004 it, and RML 2760, were run over a series of current and former routes served by the company. Here it is in Beckton blinded for the 101 to North Woolwich.

Arriva-operated RML2524 was given this very dark green Shillibeer-style livery in 2004 to mark the 175th anniversary of the start of horse buses in London. It worked on route 19 and was spotted at Finsbury Park Station on 25 July 2004.

Also painted was Arriva RM25 in Great Northern Railway horse bus colours. Both liveries were designed by students at Central St Martin's College of Art & Design. Spotted at Sadler's Wells, 1 April 2005.

To replace Trident No. 17758, which was destroyed in the 7 July 2005 bombing at Tavistock Square, Stagecoach received No. 18500. This was the first bus to the new design of Alexander Dennis Enviro400 body and was named Spirit of London to honour the dead and injured of the bombing. Initially working on route 30, it sometimes strayed on to other routes, but is seen here at the Cobham Gathering held at Wisley Airfield on 2 April 2006.

In 2008 Routemaster RM1933 received this livery to commemorate 100 years of Bow Garage where an open day was held on 28 June. It is seen having arrived at Tower Hill on heritage route 15 on 14 June.

The year 2014 was designated by TfL as the 'Year of the Bus' with several special events held. As part of this, Stagecoach repainted two vehicles. One was Alexander Dennis Dart 36343 in a red and white livery reminiscent of that given to the Dennis Lance buses of 1992 (see p. 15). It was seen here at Lewisham DLR Station on 14 June. The other was double-decker 10136 in a livery similar to that carried by L136 in 1990.

The main event of the year was the 'Year of the Bus' cavalcade from the South Bank to Regent Street on 22 June. Taking part in this and seen in Lambeth Palace Road was New Routemaster LT150, operated by London United, which was given this silver and red livery.

LT60, operated by London General, received this pre-war-style livery. It was working on route 11 in Whitehall on 22 March 2015.

In 2016 Go-Ahead-operated LT50 also received a pre-war-style livery. It was seen in service at St Paul's Cathedral in 2018.

Special Promotions

T569 in promotional lettering for the Bus & Coach Council. Waterloo Station, 23 September 1983.

The first low-loor kneeling single-deck buses entered service in 1994. Wright-bodied Dennis Lance SLF LLW3 was at Northolt on the first route, the 120, on 21 February 1994. Similar-bodied Scania buses followed in the year. All were prominently lettered to promote their credentials.

Low-floor single-deckers soon began to become the norm, followed by the first double-deck models in 1998. London United applied this image of people with buggies, shopping trolleys, etc., to some of their vehicles. DP9 also carries branding for its dedicated route, the R70 at Richmond in June 1999.

The popular pre-payment Oyster card was introduced in 2003. Stagecoach Selkent Mercedes Citaro artic 23002 was one of the vehicles painted to promote this in 2004, and was the first bendy bus to carry a special livery. Whitehall, 11 August 2004.

In 2004 forty London buses were painted to promote the Capital's bid to host the Olympic Games in 2012. Metroline Dennis Trident TAL126 was in Baker Street on 22 September.

With increasing political and public pressure over air-quality levels, TfL has been introducing hybrid buses with lower emissions. The first six came in 2006 and were Wright Electricity single-deckers based on the VDL SB120 chassis, operated by London Central on route 360. They were extensively promoted with this 'going green' imagery as on WHY6 seen near Chelsea Bridge 11 March 2007.

Experiments with alternative fuels for lower emissions have included hydrogen-powered buses giving no emissions except steam. These were operated by Tower Transit on route RV1 and this Wright-bodied VDL SB200 is at the Aldwych end of the route in July 2013.

The Red Arrow routes have been equipped with electric BYD buses with Alexander bodywork. SEe10 is one of a few that carry this green promotional livery. It was seen inside Stockwell Garage at the open day held there in October 2016.

Metroline operate five all-electric BYD double-deckers on route 98. These carry a variant of the 'leaf' imagery although these leaves look more like origami constructions! BYD1473 was seen in Oxford Street in July 2016.

LT239, operated by Stagecoach, was given this 'Ride with Pride' livery to mark the tenth anniversary of OUTbound, TfL's LGBT staff network group in 2014. Here it is at Holborn on 22 March 2015.

On show at an open day held at the Stagecoach West Ham Garage on 23 July 2016 was LT2, which had returned to service on route 38 still carrying the green livery it was given while demonstrating to First West Yorkshire in Leeds. A traditional gold underlined London Transport fleetname and cream band made a nice touch.

A promotion launched in 2018 encourages off-peak travel. Metroline VWH2121, a Wright-bodied Volvo B5LH, is one of the buses liveried for the promotion. Pictured at St Paul's in 2018.

Stagecoach 10301 was painted in this promotional livery for Macmillan Cancer Support in 2018. Allocated to Romford garage, it is usually to be found on route 86 as here in Stratford on 1 October 2018.

Contracts

Kingston Polytechnic (now Kingston University) had a contract service operated by Westlink to connect their scattered sites. Wright-bodied Dennis Dart DWL1 was parked at Kingston on 4 April 1992.

A new Tesco store opened between East Ham and Barking, and Tesco contracted Stagecoach to provide a courtesy service from Barking Station for shoppers. Dart DW159 received a dedicated livery for the service in 1994. Seen on 11 March 1995.

Another Tesco free service started in 1995 between Brent Cross Bus Station and the Tesco store. SR7 of Metroline was the dedicated vehicle for this service in August 1995. It was later replaced by SR55.

In March 1997 Stagecoach took over the contract service linking Liverpool Street Station and Canary Wharf with London City Airport. The route ran daily, but only during the hours when flights operated from the airport. Seven new Alexander-bodied Dennis Dart SLFs were provided in a dedicated blue livery. LCY3 rounds the gyratory at Aldgate on 28 March 1997. Others later ran from 1999 in a green livery for a link from the new Canning Town Bus Station.

Leaside Buses had a contract for Middlesex University. M1447, seen in Enfield on 8 April 1997, was one of seven liveried for this. This MCW Metrobus was one acquired second-hand from the Greater Manchester PTE.

Arriva operated 'The Shuttle' on behalf of the NHS. New Dennis Darts were provided in 2000 such as PDL18 seen outside Wellington House, Waterloo Road on 25 May. Previously MCW Metroriders in red, but with 'The Shuttle' fleetname, had been used.

London United DT12 received this livery for a contract service with Marks & Spencer to Kew Retail Park in 1998. It was photographed in Richmond on 15 June 2002.

For several years from 1994 Kingston sponsored a Christmas period K50 Park & Ride service between the town centre and car parks at Chessington World of Adventures. For the 2004 season, London United won the contract and provided the original Dennis Lance low-floor vehicles (see p. 71). LLW7 was seen at the Eden Street terminus with the vinyl branding that was applied. Local council austerity cuts have put paid to this and other such schemes.

London United gained the contract for the Kingston University services in 2016. VH45166 was one of seven Volvo B5LH/Wright given a temporary red and grey livery for the services until new longer buses arrived. Taken at Kingston Bus Station in September 2016.

VH45213 is one of the new dedicated buses for the services painted in the Kingston University grey livery seen in April 2017.

Go-Ahead London's commercial division gained a new contract in 2017 to provide a frequent link from Stratford City (for rail station) to Here East, a business and innovation park based in the former Olympic Press and Broadcast Centre. Three Wright StreetLites are used, and these carry dedicated vinyl in varying colours, as with WS35 seen here. A similar-liveried Dart provides back-up.

Rail Replacement

From 1 June 1993 a replacement service was operated non-stop during peak hours between Waterloo and the Bank of England while the Waterloo & City Line was closed for engineering work. Numbered 800, fourteen London Central Titans were employed. The service was sponsored by the City of London Corporation and eleven buses carried appropriate branding. T317 was near the Bank of England on 4 June.

The remaining three buses (T894, 1008/53) on the Waterloo & City Line replacement service were painted in the City of London white livery. T1008 was also seen on 4 June. The service was due to run until 9 July 1993.

A major rail replacement contract started in 1995 while work was undertaken on the East London Line from Whitechapel or Shoreditch to New Cross and New Cross Gate through Brunel's original Thames Tunnel. Stagecoach ran route ELT from Whitechapel to Surrey Quays via the Rotherhithe Tunnel, which can only take minibuses. Optare StarRider SR80 was seen leaving Surrey Quays on 14 April 1995. A double-deck route, ELX, was operated between Whitechapel and New Cross/New Cross Gate via Tower Bridge by Capital Citybus with vehicles in a similar livery. These services lasted until March 1998.

Another rail replacement job at the same time also used StarRiders but this time from Metroline. This was for North London Railways. SR67 lays over at Willesden Junction on 29 March 1996.

From June 1997 new limited-stop route TL1 ran between Wimbledon and West Croydon on Mondays to Saturdays. This was to replace the Connex train service between these points, which was closed for conversion to the Croydon Tramlink. Ikarus-bodied DAFs were used, released by Grey-Green after they had been replaced by new low-floor Darts. Livery was red and white – the colours of the new trams that replaced them from 2000. On 24 June 1999 DIB5 awaits any potential passengers at West Croydon Bus Station.

In December 2007 the LUL East London Line closed in preparation for its transfer to London Overground and extension to Dalston. A series of bus routes replaced parts of the line and this Marshall-bodied Dart was employed on the ELW at Whitechapel in August 2008. Rail services resumed in May 2010.

Overall Advertising

From 1969 to the early 1970s, and then in 1983–84, several Routemasters were treated to overall advertising liveries. Initially these would have been hand painted. Commercial advertising made a regular comeback from 2004 – ironically just as company liveries were being tightened up to predominantly red. Nowadays adverts are applied in vinyl wraps and are often short-term commercial promotions.

RML2492 received this livery for Underwood developing and printing in 1984. However the London Buses authorities were somewhat ambivalent to overall advertising and this one put them off it for twenty years. It was seen working on route 11 in Whitehall on 7 July 1984.

One recent advert that has been around for longer than most is that on LT100, liveried in 2014 to mark sixty years of the Fender Stratocaster electric guitar. Here it is seen in 2016 on route 390 emerging from the back streets having just departed from Euston Station.

Coaching and Private Hire

When London Buses Ltd replaced London Transport they took a more commercial approach and developed coaching, contracts and private hire work. A Tours & Charter division was established, which was renamed London Coaches in 1987. This was also responsible for the Round London Sightseeing Tour and would become the first company to be privatised. The other bus operating companies set up in 1989 also developed coaching. Vehicles used on such work were not subject to the same stringent livery code as buses. When the bus companies were privatised this continued at first, but as they were later absorbed by the major national groups some ceased this work in line with their parent company policy.

London Transport bought five single-door Leyland Titans from West Midlands PTE in 1984 and had them fitted with coach seating. In 1987 T1128 was working with London Forest in this Forest Ranger livery when it was an entrant at the Southend Rally. With the demise of London Forest it passed to East London and was repainted similar to T512 (see p. 88) by 1989. This vehicle is now preserved and has repainted to the style seen here.

A short-lived initiative saw London Buses start joint services to Birmingham (with West Midlands) and Eastbourne (with Eastbourne Corporation) in 1986 under the London Liner name. When these ended, the vehicles were re-lettered as London Coaches for private hire and tour work. Leyland Olympian/East Lancs coach C201 DYE, originally for the Eastbourne service, was on tour duty when noted on London Bridge on 18 March 1990.

In 1989 London Forest acquired this former London Country Green Line TP14, a Leyland Tiger TRCTL11/2R with Plaxton Paramount C53F body. It was an entrant at the North Weald rally.

East London Coaches T512 lost its roof in 1988 and was rebuilt as an open-topper. It had received this East London Coaches livery by 1991 when it was photographed making a rare appearance on normal bus work passing Wanstead Flats on 1 October 1991. Under Stagecoach ownership it was later transferred from London to work in the Lake District.

East London Leyland Titan T63 was fitted with coach seating and repainted in East London Coaches livery shortly before the company was sold to Stagecoach. Seen in Romford in May 1995. Like many vehicles used on such duties it has gained a non-age-specific registration number, originally carried on RML890.

Corporate bus-style livery for this Volvo B10M with Jonckheere bodywork of Stagecoach East London, seen in Brighton. Stagecoach closed down their coaching operations in March 2007.

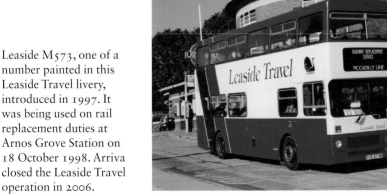

Leaside M573, one of a number painted in this Leaside Travel livery, introduced in 1997. It was being used on rail replacement duties at Arnos Grove Station on 18 October 1998. Arriva closed the Leaside Travel operation in 2006.

Selkent Olympians L260–3 were fitted with coach seats and painted as part of the Selkent Travel fleet when delivered in 1987. L261 received a red and gold livery and was an entrant in the 1987 British Coach Rally held on Brighton seafront, 26 April 1987. It has had the 2 CLT registration transferred from RM1002.

Selkent Travel Olympian L260 was at Thurrock Lakeside working a shopper's excursion route 750 on 18 April 1992.

London Central T803 was converted to open-top. Here it works a summer extra on route 12 and was noted at Oxford Circus on 13 August 1993.

MTL London Northern open-top M804 was given the Sightseers livery adopted for coaches in 1995. It was used on the London Zoo service Z1.

Go-Ahead London continue to run an extensive 'Commercial Services' fleet of some fifty vehicles on special services, private hires, excursions, etc. WVL93 is a convertible open-top Volvo B7TL, seen here working local trips as part of an open day at Stockwell Garage in 2014.

Go-Ahead London E284 is one of a pair of Alexander Dennis E40D with Enviro400 (MMC) bodies bought new for the Commercial Services fleet in 2017. These carry the older-style livery with dark skirt discontinued on service buses. It was at Alexandra Palace on 27 March 2017 working a connecting service to Wood Green for the Model Railway Exhibition.

Some Darts in the Commercial Services fleet carry an ivory and purple livery, such as PHD271 seen at Alexandra Palace on 23 March 2019. Some Mercedes Citaros, now relegated to driver training, carry the same livery.

London United had a commercial unit United Motorcoaches. A grey and red livery was used with 'United Transit' fleetnames as seen on open-top Leyland Olympian OA332 at Shepherds Bush garage in 2016. The United Motorcoaches identity was dropped in 2018 after National Express work was lost and buses like the Olympians were too old to meet London emissions standards.

Trainers and Other Non-passenger Uses

Vehicles used for training are exempt from the livery restrictions imposed on those in passenger service. With the increasing difficulty in recruiting sufficient drivers experienced by many of the companies, some quite elaborate liveries have appeared to attract attention. Others carried overall advertising during the period when this was not permitted on service buses.

Centrewest were using RMC1492 as a dedicated trainer when it was entered in the 1993 North Weald Rally. The yellow blind reads 'RMC1492 30th anniversary 1962–1992'.

This London General B20 Fleetline had been adapted as a trainer and renumbered DMT2476. On this occasion it was spotted in Brighton on 3 May 1992 – on hire to Brighton & Hove perhaps?

London United M1022 had been adapted for training when it was seen here at Cobham in 2002.

First CentreWest M338 had become a dedicated trainer when recorded here at Hyde Park Corner in 2002.

This Go-Ahead London General Volvo Olympian in Whitehall in 2004 lists the locations of the company's London garages in its promotional lettering.

One of the original low-floor buses for London, Stagecoach 28629 was a Wright-bodied Scania, which worked route 101. By 2005 it had become a training vehicle in this mauve livery.

Former Leyland National LS334 was converted to become a London Transport Museum sales bus. It was used at Covent Garden as a temporary replacement for the museum shop while the museum was being refurbished. 15 May 1993.

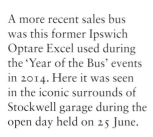

A more recent sales bus was this former Ipswich Optare Excel used during the 'Year of the Bus' events in 2014. Here it was seen in the iconic surrounds of Stockwell garage during the open day held on 25 June.

Acknowledgements and Bibliography

Baker, Michael H.C., *London Transport Since 1933* (Shepperton: Ian Allen, 2000).

Batten, Malcolm, *London's Buses: The Colourful Era 1985–2005* (Stroud: Amberley, 2018).

Carr, Ken, *Campaign: London's Advertising Buses 1969–2016* (Boreham: Visions International, 2016).

King, Nicholas, *London Bus Handbook Part 1: London Buses Ltd* (Harrow Weald: Capital Transport, various editions, 1990s).

Lane, Kevin, *London Half-cab Farewell* (Hersham: Ian Allan, 2009).

Reed, John, *London Buses Past and Present* (Harrow Weald: Capital Transport, 1988).

Wharmby, Matthew & Rixon, Geoff, *Routemaster Omnibus* (Hersham: Ian Allan, 2008).

Buses (Hersham: Ian Allen, 1970)

Various publications, including fleet lists and newsletters by the London Omnibus Traction Society. This is the principal society for enthusiasts of London Transport and its successors, and anyone with an interest in the London bus scene past and present is recommended to join. www.lots.org.uk.